Code Crafting

FSC
www.fsc.org
MIX
Papper från
ansvarsfulla källor
Paper from
responsible sources
FSC® C105338

Code Crafting no. 5

Never Done:

The Double Non-Closure of Software Work

Set Lonnert
with AI Coöperation

All trademarks are the property of their respective owners.

Cover photograph is by Set Lonnert and depict Iceland, 2026.

Author: Set Lonnert 2026
AI Support: Multiple large language models

Publisher: BoD · Books on Demand, Östermalmstorg 1, 114 42 Stockholm, Sweden, bod@bod.se
Print: Libri Plureos GmbH, Friedensallee 273, 22763 Hamburg, Germany
ISBN: 978-91-8134-234-5

Contents

Introduction: The Two Openings

Take two ordinary moments from a working week, before any theory is brought to bear on them, and notice what each one quietly says about the medium.

The first. A programmer writes a small function and gives one of its parameters a convenient default—an empty list, to be filled if the caller supplies nothing. The code is clear, the tests are green, the type checker raises no objection, and it ships. Months later a bug surfaces that makes no sense until it does: the list was created once, when the function was defined, and every call that trusted the default has been quietly sharing and adding to the same list ever since. Nothing was mistyped. The type discipline that was supposed to catch errors of exactly this weight looked straight at the function and passed it, because no rule of that kind decides every case it will meet. There is code the rule should forbid, and does not, and no amount of care in writing the rule closes the gap—a claim this book will later sharpen from a complaint into a theorem.

The second. A service that shipped clean a year ago—every test green, no known defect—is left untouched: no new features, no edits, not a line changed. Return to it now and it will not run. Nothing *in* it moved; everything *under* it did. A dependency advanced, a certificate lapsed, an operating system shifted beneath it, a protocol it speaks acquired a version it does not. The program worked only for as long as someone kept reproducing it against a world that refused to hold still. Left alone, it did not sit finished on a shelf like a chair in a dry room. It rotted.

These are the book's two subjects, and its single claim about them is that neither ever closes. The rule does not close: no type, no specification, no convention covers all the cases it will govern. The artefact does not close: software is never a thing one finishes, only a thing one keeps in being. Everything difficult about the trade, this book will argue, follows from the pair.

Two openings, not one

The first discipline, held from this page to the last, is to see that these are *two* openings and to refuse the temptation to make them one. They are not the same fact wearing two coats.

The first is a fact about **rules**. A rule that governs code—a type discipline, a specification, a house convention—has a settled core of cases it plainly decides and a margin of cases it does not, and the margin is not a defect of drafting that a more careful author would have closed. For the formal heart of the matter it is a limit no procedure escapes; the gap is a theorem, not a shortfall, and chapter 2 is where that is shown. Call this the **logical** opening: a property of what any rule can cover.

The second is a fact about **artefacts**. A program is less like a built object than like a score that must be performed or a recipe that must be cooked: it delivers nothing by merely existing, only by being enacted again, and its upkeep has the form of labor—cyclical, consumed in the doing, leaving nothing that stands unless the doing continues. Chapter 3 is where that form is named and its one honest complication faced. Call this the **temporal** opening: a property of how an artefact persists in time.

One opening is logical and one is temporal; one concerns what a rule reaches, the other how a thing endures. They are two lenses on one condition, and the book never claims they are one essence. To say they are secretly the same phenomenon would be the easy pun that dissolves the whole argument into wordplay, and the reader should hold the book to its refusal of it. The openings meet at exactly one place—a single, observable, datable site—and finding that place is the book's hinge, promised at the end of this introduction and kept in chapter 4.

What this book is not

Because the subject invites grander company than it can keep, the fence goes up on the first page. This is not a philosophy of incompleteness. Gödel is not pressed into service as a metaphor; entropy is not invoked; nothing here leans on an analogy to decay, or finitude, or mortality. Those are borrowed profundities, and the argument is built to run without a single one of them. Nor is this a theory of meaning, or of law, or of the being of the technical object—though it borrows, narrowly and with the borrowing flagged each time, a term from the philosophy of language and a distinction from legal theory, taking the tool and leaving the system it came from.

What it is, is smaller and firmer: an account of what a maker does in a medium where neither the rules nor the things ever come to rest. The test every paragraph must pass is correspondingly concrete. Each claim is leashed to a named artefact—this lint rule, that suppression comment, this rotting dependency, that on-call rotation, the mutable default just described—and a sentence that cannot be tied back to one, however true it sounds, has failed the book's own standard and is cut. The reader is entitled to ask of any page: which verdict, on which piece of real code, does this change?

What this book claims

Set against that fence, the positive claims are few, and each is meant to be held to account. First: the two openings are one condition seen twice, not two facts that merely co-occur—the argument stands or falls on their being at once genuinely distinct and genuinely joined. Second: they meet at a place one can date and point to, the commit in which a custom kept by hand becomes a rule a machine enforces. Third: that enclosure closes nothing—it relocates the margin it was meant to remove, opening a fresh frontier of discretion at the new rule's edge (chapter 4, chapter 5). Fourth: the low standing of maintenance is not merely a prejudice to be scolded away but follows from the form of the work—labor in the exact sense taken up in chapter 3—set over a logical opening no upkeep can write shut. Fifth: one can therefore answer this condition well without reversing it, a distinction—*adequate*, not *successful*—the book means to earn rather than assume. Sixth: the ethics of the craft live not in finishing, which no one can do, but in the light under which the discretion that survives every rule is left—exercised on a record and open to a reason, or hidden. And the whole result is indifferent to tooling, the newest filler included: a faster guess over the openings is not a way through them. Each claim is argued below against named code; none is asked to be granted here.

The companions, declined

This is the fifth and final of the *Code Crafting* essays, and it is written to be read alone. Two of the earlier volumes—among them *The Worldless Machine* (no. 3)—arrived, from the side of mind, at the thought that to apply a concept is already to legislate at its margin; a fourth built and studied the type systems whose failure to close this book takes as its starting fact rather than its conclusion. A reader who knows those books will hear the argument rhyme with them. A reader who does not loses nothing that is needed here: no step below depends on them, and where one is echoed the echo is marked. The self-containment is not a courtesy. It is the same discipline as the leash—an argument that has to import a prior book to stand up has not yet been made.

The hinge

One promise remains, and the book is staked on keeping it. If the two openings are genuinely distinct—one logical, one temporal—then the interesting question is not whether both are real but whether they ever touch, and where. They do, at one place, and it is a place any programmer can point to: the commit in which a custom that everyone had been observing by hand hardens into a rule a machine now enforces—the afternoon the folklore against mutable defaults becomes `pylint`'s `dangerous-default-value` wired into a build that fails without it. That one act is both things at once. Seen from the side of the rule, a piece of the undecided margin is annexed into the settled core. Seen from the side of the day, a piece of endlessly repeated labor is set down, for once, as work that stands. Not an analogy between two events—the same commit, under two descriptions. Chapter 4 is where that identity is shown, and it is the reason this is one book and not two essays that happen to share a shelf.

But that is the destination, and the trade does not begin there. It begins, almost universally, by talking as though it makes finished things—as though 'done' were a state software occupies rather than one it passes through. If both openings are real, why does the craft narrate itself as a maker of durable, completed objects? That is the question the first chapter takes up.

Chapter 1

The Craft That Thinks It Finishes

1.1 A vocabulary of making

Programmers describe what they do in the vocabulary of making. They build; they speak of architecture and of foundations, of a system *constructed* with care, of a library *crafted* well, of code that is *clean* the way a joint is clean. Donald Knuth called the discipline an art and gave his life's work the title *The Art of Computer Programming*, on the working assumption that a program, like a proof or a well-set page, could be brought to a condition in which it was simply *right* and needed no more done to it.[1] The movements the trade has been fondest of—craftsmanship, clean code, literate programming—are variations on one picture: the programmer as a maker of durable, finishable things, and the good programmer as one who finishes them well.

The picture is not foolish, and this book does not begin by mocking it. Richard Sennett's craftsman is defined by the desire to do a job well for its own sake, a desire prior to and deeper than any reward the job returns; and that desire is unmistakably present at the programmer's bench—in the reworking of a function that already passes its tests until it is not merely correct but *clear*, in the satisfaction of the abstraction that finally sits right, in the small grief of leaving a module worse than one would like

[1]The same assumption runs through the literature the trade holds dearest: the 'software craftsmanship' movement—whose founding manual, Andrew Hunt and David Thomas's *The Pragmatic Programmer* (Addison-Wesley, 1999), recasts programming as a journeyman-to-master craft—the cult of 'clean code', the long affection for literate programming. What they share is not a doctrine but a picture—of the programmer as a maker of durable, finishable things.

because the sprint is over.[2] The impulse to build something that stands is genuine, it is central to the trade, and the argument that follows keeps it to the end. What the argument does not keep is the belief that travels with it.

1.2 Two things the self-image fuses

For the self-image is not one claim but two, welded together so tightly that the trade rarely notices the weld. The first is a claim about a *desire*: that the programmer wants to make durable things well. The second is a claim about the *medium*: that software is a material in which durable things, once well made, stay made—that a program can reach the condition of the finished chair or the printed book, the condition in which the maker sets down the tool and walks away and the thing remains as left. The first claim is true. The second is false, and almost everything difficult about the trade lives in the gap the weld conceals.

Separate them and the difficulty comes into focus. The desire to finish and the possibility of finishing are not the same, and a medium can grant the first appetite while withholding the second satisfaction forever. That is software's situation. The programmer wants, rightly and craftsman-like, to bring the thing to a state of completion; the medium never lets the state arrive. 'Done' is not a condition software occupies. It is a condition software *passes through*, on its way to needing attention again—and the whole of this book is an account of why the passing-through is structural rather than a failure of diligence.

One qualification must be made at once, because without it the chapter would be attacking a straw man. Not everyone in the trade holds the second claim; a large and clear-eyed engineering tradition has denied it in print for two generations. David Parnas drew module boundaries around *anticipated changes* and later gave the slow spoiling of neglected code its exact name, *software aging*; Meir Lehman made continual change the First Law of software evolution; Bertrand Meyer's open/closed principle and Kent Beck's slogan to *embrace change* turned designing-for-impermanence into a discipline taught to beginners.[3] So the belief this chapter takes apart is not the field's considered engineering knowledge. It is the craft-*romance*—the picture carried in the vocabulary of chairs, cathedrals, and clean joints—which persists *beside* that knowledge and quietly contradicts it, in the same practitioners, on the same afternoon. And there

[2] Richard Sennett, *The Craftsman* (Yale University Press, 2008). The book borrows Sennett here for one purpose only—to establish that the making-impulse is real and worth honouring—and does not take up his larger account of skill, which is chapter 3's concern.

[3] David Parnas, 'On the Criteria to Be Used in Decomposing Systems into Modules' (1972) and 'Software Aging' (1994); Meir Lehman, 'Programs, Life Cycles, and Laws of Software Evolution' (1980); Bertrand Meyer, *Object-Oriented Software Construction* (1988), for the open/closed principle; Kent Beck, *Extreme Programming Explained: Embrace Change* (1999). The engineering field has never needed to be told that software changes.

is a difference between the two that the whole book turns on. The engineering tradition treats change as a problem to be *managed*: anticipated, hidden behind an interface, tamed by good structure. This book treats it as a *condition* to be understood—not a difficulty that better architecture dissolves but a permanent feature of the medium that architecture can only relocate. What the engineers know it does not dispute; what it adds is that their managing never terminates, and the reason why.

One voice in that tradition stood closer to a condition than to a problem, and it is the oldest of them. Half a century ago Frederick Brooks, surveying the same trade, drew a line between software's *accidental* difficulties—the ones better tools and languages do dissolve—and its *essential* ones, which inhere in the nature of the thing and which he judged irreducible: no single advance, he predicted, would ever cut the labour of building software by an order of magnitude, because the hard part is not the making but the conceiving, and the conceiving does not get easier.[4] Brooks reported the irreducibility as a brute fact of engineering and left it there. This book takes the same fact and asks what *kind* of difficulty could be essential in that way—and finds not one answer but two, a rule that will not close and an artefact that will not rest, which is the double subject of everything that follows. The diagnosis, in other words, is old. The account is what is new.

1.3 The exception that keeps the rule: TEX

There is, famously, one program that nearly finished, and it is worth dwelling on, because it is the exception that shows precisely what completion in software would cost. Knuth's TEX—the typesetting system that composed this page—was declared essentially complete by its author decades ago. Its version number no longer increments toward the next feature; it converges, digit by digit, on the number π, and will be frozen at π on Knuth's death. No new capability is added. Reported defects are corrected, ever more rarely, and the correction is treated as an embarrassment rather than a release. TEX is, as nearly as any real program has ever been, a *finished* thing.[5]

[4] Frederick P. Brooks, Jr., 'No Silver Bullet: Essence and Accidents of Software Engineering' (1986), collected in the anniversary edition of *The Mythical Man-Month* (Addison-Wesley, 1995; orig. 1975). The essence/accident distinction and the irreducibility claim are Brooks's; the book takes them as testimony from inside engineering and declines the surrounding productivity forecast, which is not its subject. Where Brooks names the difficulty essential, chapters 2 and 3 say of what two kinds.

[5] The completeness is literal to the point of publication. Knuth issued the entire source of TEX as a book—*TEX: The Program* (1986), a literate program written in his WEB system—and placed it effectively in the public domain, under the single condition that no altered version bear the name. The finished artefact is thus not a running binary but a canonical printed text: the completion is embodied as a *description*, which is the only form in which, as chapter 3 argues, software ever really stands still.

But look at what finishing it required. TeX did not arrive at completion by satisfying the medium's ordinary conditions; it arrived there by *stepping out of them.* Knuth froze the specification and refused all extension. He wrote the system to depend on as little beneath it as possible, and defined the little it did depend on so exactly that the ground could not shift under it. He declined, deliberately and against enormous pressure, to let TeX grow into the uses people found for it—those became other programs, built on top, that are not finished and never will be. TeX is complete because Knuth built, by main force, a small motionless world around it and then forbade the world to move. Completion in software was available exactly once, to the person willing to freeze the substrate and refuse the future—which is to say it was available only by *opting out* of the condition the medium imposes on everything that stays in use. The exception does not soften the rule. It states the rule's price.

1.4 A memory of another workshop

The ordinary artefact does not get TeX's dispensation. It sits on a substrate that moves—a language that revises, a dependency that advances, an operating system, a protocol, a hardware assumption—and it keeps working only by being carried along, which is to say by being worked on again. A library left alone for five years is not preserved, like a chair in a dry room; it is *spoiled*, having stood still while everything it rested on walked away. And the maker who returns to improve it does not add to a finished thing the way a mason adds a course; she consumes what she built last year as the raw material of what she builds this year, feeding her own prior work into the refactor that supersedes it. The output of the craft is, with unnerving regularity, the *input* of the same craft a year on.

The self-image, then, is a memory of another workshop. Its images—the chair, the printed page, the cathedral the software 'architect' unconsciously invokes—are drawn from crafts whose materials hold their shape once worked, and imported into a craft whose material does not. This is why the picture is a memory and not a description: it recalls, accurately, the maker's desire, and attributes to the new medium a durability that belonged to the old one. The danger, having said so, is not that we will believe the picture but that we will over-correct into its sentimental opposite—the lament, as old as Ruskin and Morris, that the machine has killed the honest craft and left only drudgery.[6] That lament keeps the grief and loses the impulse, which is the wrong half to keep. This book does the reverse. It grants that the thing is never finished and holds on, all the way through, to the desire that it be well made anyway.

[6]John Ruskin, 'The Nature of Gothic', in *The Stones of Venice* (1853); William Morris after him. Their diagnosis—that industrial production severs the maker from the dignity of finished work—is the nineteenth-century original of the complaint this book is often mistaken for. It is kept here strictly as a warning: the lament curdled into nostalgia, and a book that wants to keep the making-impulse must not also inherit the mourning.

1.5 Where the denial comes from

So the craft's self-image is half right and half wrong, and we have found the weld: the desire to make durable work is real, the belief that the medium lets the work be finished is false, and the trade experiences the two as one because it inherited them as one. Everything after this is an account of the false half—not to debunk the craft, but to say what the medium withholds and why, so that the true half can be practised without the illusion that used to accompany it.

And the withholding has two sources, not one, which is why the book has the shape it does. A thing can fail to be finished because the *rule* that governs it never closes—because no specification, no type, no convention ever settles all the cases the thing will meet—and it can fail to be finished because the *artefact* itself never comes to rest—because it decays against a moving world and must be perpetually remade. These are two different ways of not being done, and software suffers both at once. Take them one at a time, and in that order. First the rule.

Chapter 2

The Rule That Cannot Close

2.1 The rule that admits what it forbids

Begin with the compiler, because it is the strictest rule we have and therefore the most instructive when it fails. A compiler is, on the face of it, the very image of a rule that leaves no room: the program either type-checks or it does not, either parses or does not, and no plea, context, or intention alters the verdict. If any rule anywhere compels its own application without the play that Wittgenstein found in every human rule—the gap between the rule and the act of following it—surely it is this one.[1]

And yet the compiler admits, without a murmur, code that every competent programmer knows to be wrong. A function given a mutable value as its default parameter type-checks perfectly and does the wrong thing on its second call; a cast that discards a qualifier, an integer that overflows, a pointer read just past the end of an array: the rule runs, returns its verdict, and the verdict is silent on the question that matters. The strictest rule we have has a region where it decides nothing—and it is not a small or exotic region. It is where most of the day's real judgement happens. So the pattern we will find everywhere is already here at the hardest case: a rule has a *settled core*, where it runs mechanically and binds, and a *penumbra*, where it falls silent and something outside it must decide. The name for the penumbra is old. Friedrich Waismann called it the *open texture* of a concept; H. L. A. Hart carried the picture into law and drew the conclusion that in the penumbra the judge does not find the rule's answer but supplies one.[2]

[1]Ludwig Wittgenstein, *Philosophical Investigations*, §§185–242. The compiler is of interest here as the limiting case of his problem: the rule that appears to compel absolutely. The interest is in watching even it leave room. The book borrows the point and does not stay to adjudicate the rule-following paradox itself.

[2]Friedrich Waismann, 'Verifiability' (1945), for the term; H. L. A. Hart, *The Concept of Law* (1961), ch. VII, for the core-and-penumbra picture and the claim that at the margin the judge leg-

2.2 Four doors to the same room

It would be convenient, and it would be false, to say that the penumbra is one thing. A rule falls silent for several different reasons, and candour about the difference is what keeps this argument from becoming a pun.

A rule can give out through *vagueness*: a convention like 'keep functions small' or 'handle errors near their source' has a clear centre and no edge, and two careful readers will place its boundary in different rows. It can give out through *unforeseeability*, in Waismann's original sense: a rule framed for the cases its authors could imagine meets one they could not, and simply has nothing to say. It can give out by *fiat*: the C standard does not overlook the behaviour of a signed overflow or an out-of-bounds read—it names these cases and declares them *undefined*, deliberately handing them back to the compiler so the optimiser has room to work.

```
int f(int x) { return x + 1 > x; }

        // "obviously" true...
        // ...but signed overflow is undefined,
        // so the compiler may assume it, and
        // fold the whole thing to 1
```

And it can give out through *undecidability*: the question 'does this program halt?', or more generally 'does this program have this behaviour?', is perfectly precise and admits no general procedure that answers it.

These are four different reasons, not four names for one reason. Vagueness is not unforeseeability; a deliberate 'undefined' is almost the opposite of an oversight; and undecidability is a fact of mathematics, not of drafting. What they share is not a nature but a *consequence*: in each case the rule does not decide, and a decision the rule does not make must be made by something outside it. That shared consequence—not any shared essence—is the subject of this chapter. The distinction will matter again, because the four doors do not all close the same way, and one of them does not close at all.

2.3 The door that is a theorem

Take the fourth door seriously, because it does something the first three cannot: it turns the penumbra from a contingency into a theorem. One might hope that vagueness could be drafted away with enough care, or unforeseeability outrun by a sufficiently far-sighted author; these are hopes about effort. Undecidability is not. Rice's

islates. Both are borrowed for a single move—the shape of the gap—and neither's larger system is taken up here.

theorem states that every non-trivial property of the behaviour a program computes—every property that some programs have and others lack—is undecidable: there is no procedure that, given an arbitrary program, always terminates with the right yes or no.[3] The halting problem is its most famous instance.

What this forecloses is a specific and popular dream: that the penumbra of a type system or a specification is a temporary embarrassment, a measure of how far our tools still fall short, to be closed by the next, more complete type discipline or the next, more total specification. For the general case, it cannot be closed, and the impossibility is not practical but proven. A type system strong enough to admit every good program and reject every bad one, deciding of an arbitrary program whether it has the property in question, is not merely hard to build; it cannot exist.[4] The penumbra of the formal rule is not a shortfall in rigour. It is a theorem about rigour's limit.

Two disciplines on this, so the theorem constrains rather than decorates. First, Rice closes only the fourth door. It says nothing about whether a human convention is vague, and a book that waved the halting problem at the difficulty of 'keep functions small' would be committing the equivocation section 2.2 was at pains to avoid. What the theorem gives us is narrower and sufficient: at least one source of the penumbra is provably ineliminable, which is enough to make non-closure a condition of the medium and not a stage in its improvement. Second, the theorem bites only on the general, arbitrary case; particular programs can of course be proven to halt, and the whole discipline of verification lives in that space. The point is not that nothing can be proved. It is that the space of the provable has a boundary no amount of effort moves, and the rule gives out at that boundary by necessity.

It is worth marking which of the book's two openings this is, because the two are not equally acknowledged by the trade. The engineering tradition chapter 1 invoked has long known that the *artefact* changes—designing for change is its watchword, and chapter 3 takes up that opening in full. The *rule*'s non-closure is the quieter one. A practitioner can embrace the impermanence of the thing and still suppose the specification governing it might, with enough rigour, be made complete—that the penumbra is a debt rigour will one day pay off. Rice is the reason that second supposition is idle. The artefacts restlessness is a fact the field has metabolised; the rule's incompleteness, being a theorem rather than a difficulty, is the one it more often hopes to out-engineer.

[3] H. G. Rice, 'Classes of recursively enumerable sets and their decision problems', *Transactions of the AMS* 74 (1953); the halting problem is its most famous instance. The result is used here for one purpose only—to establish that the penumbra of the formal rule is permanent, not to expound the theory of computation—and it is the one place in the book where a formal result carries the argument directly rather than illustrating it.

[4] Nor is the gap closed by a statistical code generator. Such a model guesses over the penumbra rather than deciding it, and Rice's theorem binds the guesser exactly as it binds the type system: no procedure, learned or programmed, decides an undecidable property. A model relocates *who* fills the gap; it does not abolish the gap, and the difference between a filler that leaves reasons and one that leaves none is taken up later.

2.4 How a codebase governs what its rules leave open

If the rule does not decide the penumbral case, something does, and in a working codebase that something is an unwritten custom—'how we do it here'—enforced not by the compiler but by the reviewer, the convention, the accumulated sense of the project. This custom is more structured than it looks, and the temptation is to reach for the nearest well-theorised model of unwritten rules built up from decisions, and to say that code review *is* case law. It is worth seeing how far that holds, because the places it breaks are findings, not failures.

Three features carry across cleanly. A review enforces a *ratio* and scatters *obiter*: the binding part is the principle it stands on—'no shared mutable state across these threads'—and the rest is the reviewer's passing preference about a name, which no one treats as law. Reviewers *distinguish* constantly and in the lawyer's exact sense: 'that convention was for the synchronous path; this is async, so it does not govern here.' And a codebase honours something very like *per incuriam*: a change that slipped through against an established convention is treated as a mistake to be corrected, not as a precedent to be followed—'that got merged by accident; do not cite it.'

But press on the model and it gives way at three joints, and the giving-way is the real content. There is no *stare decisis*: no doctrine obliges a reviewer to follow prior practice, and one who ignores it faces no appeal—the bindingness is sociological, a matter of standing and pressure, not an institutional rule that says precedent binds. There is no *reporter*: the overwhelming majority of these decisions vanish into stale review threads no one reopens, so the precedent survives not as a citable, reasoned opinion but as the code itself, or as tacit habit. And because it survives as the code, statute and case-law *collapse into one text*: in law the rule and the record of past decisions are distinct documents, whereas 'do it the way the codebase does it' reads rule and precedent off the same lines, fusing what law is at pains to keep apart. So the precise claim is not that code review is case law. It is that a codebase carries an unwritten *customary order*—a common law without courts, without reporters, and without *stare decisis*, in which the code serves at once as statute and as case record. That is a weaker claim, and a truer one, and the difference between them—who fills the penumbra, and whether they must give reasons or leave a record—is a thread this book picks up again when the technical question has become an ethical one.

That thread has lately acquired an extreme occupant. More and more the penumbra is filled not by a reviewer who can be asked for a reason but by a statistical model trained on past code, which returns the customary answer and can give no account of it—the reporter-less custom carried to the point where not even the code remains as the record. What that does to the ethics of the penumbra is chapter 5's to work out; here it is enough to note that the discretion the rule cedes is coming to be exercised by something that leaves neither reasons nor a trail.

2.5 The completeness fantasy

We can now name a recurring dream and say why it fails. In one form it is the verification maximalist's: prove everything, specify totally, and drive the penumbra to nothing. In another it is the enthusiast's for 'law as code'—render the rules of a contract, or a statute, as a program that executes itself and leaves no room for the judge.[5] The two are one dream in two settings: that the open texture of a rule is an accident of insufficient rigour, and that enough rigour abolishes it. Section 2.3 answered the dream for the formal door with a theorem; and the customary order of section 2.4 shows that even where the penumbra *can* be legislated—even where a convention is written down and enforced—the writing-down does not abolish the penumbra so much as relocate it, a claim this book will make good later, at the exact site where custom hardens into a rule. The completeness fantasy fails not for want of effort. It fails because the incompleteness it hopes to overcome is the structure of a rule, not a defect in this one.

2.6 What the rule hands to the artefact

So the first source of the medium's unfinishability is established, and it is the rule: no specification, type, or convention closes over all its cases; at least one reason it cannot is a theorem; and the codebase governs the remainder by an unwritten custom that binds without a court. The obvious response is the one the chapters that follow must reckon with—if the penumbra is filled by custom, then write the custom down, legislate the margin, harden the practice into a rule and close the gap by hand, case by case, forever.

It is a real move, and part of this book is devoted to what happens when it is made. But it cannot *finish*, and the reason it cannot lies outside the rule entirely. To legislate the penumbra is itself work, and work performed on a thing that will not hold still: every convention written down is a convention about an artefact that is already changing underneath the writing, throwing up new cases faster than the old ones can be enclosed. The rule's incompleteness we have now seen. The other incompleteness—the one that makes legislating the rule an endless rather than a finite task—belongs not to the rule but to the thing the rule is about, which is never done. That is the second opening, and the subject of chapter 3.

[5] The dream is not hypothetical. The Continental codification tradition—the Roman–Napoleonic line of codified statute (as in, say, Sweden)—is its natural experiment, run for two centuries against the English case law built up decision by decision. The finding is not that codification closed the penumbra where precedent left it open: both traditions confront open texture, as Hart insisted a rule always must. It is that writing the answer down in advance moves *who* fills the margin, and *when*—the legislator before the case rather than the judge within it—without removing the margin. The codes drafted most aggressively to spare the judge all discretion are the ones that had to grow the most around themselves: general clauses, teleological interpretation, an admitted doctrine of gaps. Codification relocates the penumbra; it does not abolish it.

Chapter 3

The Machine That Is Never Done

3.1 The thing that will not stay made

Chapter 2 found the first way software refuses to finish: the rule that governs it never closes. This chapter finds the second, and it is a different kind of refusal—not a rule failing to reach every case, but the artefact failing to stay made once the rule has done all it can. Take a library that is, by every standard chapter 2 allowed, done—correct, clear, well reviewed, its penumbra as settled as care can make it—and leave it alone. Do not touch it for five years. What you return to is not what you left. The language beneath it has revised; a dependency has moved on and taken its interface with it; the operating system has changed an assumption the code quietly relied on; a protocol it speaks has a new version. The library did nothing, and that is what spoiled it. It stood still while everything it rested on walked away.

This is worth stating as sharply as the theorem in chapter 2, because it is just as structural and far more familiar—indeed it has been the settled finding of the engineering tradition chapter 1 named, held there for two generations, not a philosopher's import into a field that would not recognise it.[1] A program keeps working only by being carried along a moving substrate, and being carried along means being worked on

[1] Meir Lehman made it his First Law of software evolution: an E-type program—one embedded in the world it serves—must be continually adapted or grow progressively less satisfactory ('Programs, Life Cycles, and Laws of Software Evolution', *Proc. IEEE*, 1980; with Belady, *Program Evolution*, 1985). David Parnas named the decay of code left to itself *software aging*, tracing it both to a program's failure to keep pace with a moving world and to the structural damage of repeated change ('Software Aging', ICSE, 1994). The fact of continual change is theirs and the field's; what this chapter adds is the reading of it as *labor-form*, and the account of why the trade holds in contempt the very upkeep the fact makes unavoidable.

again. 'Done' is therefore not a state software occupies but one it passes through; the finished thing is finished only until the ground it stands on shifts, which it always does. We met the single exception in chapter 1: Knuth's $\TeX$ is complete because Knuth froze the world beneath it and forbade that world to move. Completion required stepping out of the medium's condition. Everything that stays in the medium inherits the condition instead, and the condition is this: the artefact does not come to rest. Call it the temporal opening, to mark it off from the logical one, and note at once that they are different in kind—the rule cannot cover every case; the artefact cannot stop needing attention—so that nothing in this chapter licenses the reader, or the author, to treat the two as one.

3.2 Labor, work, and a frank concession

To say what kind of refusal this is, one distinction earns its keep, and only one. Hannah Arendt separated *work* from *labor*. Work is fabrication: the making of durable artefacts that outlast the act of making and stand together as a world one can leave and come back to—the table, the building, the book. Labor is the cyclical activity that sustains life's process and is consumed in the doing, leaving nothing durable behind and having always to be done again—the meal cooked and eaten, the room cleaned and dirtied.[2] The mark of work is that it *stands*; the mark of labor is that it must be *re-enacted*.

Now the concession, made in the open because the good faith of the chapter depends on it. Software maintenance is not labor in Arendt's strict sense. Her labor is bound to biological necessity, the body's metabolism with nature; a rotting dependency is not hunger, and the on-call engineer is not tilling a field to stay alive. A reader who holds Arendt to the letter is right to refuse the identity, and this book does not need it. What it needs is the *form*. The upkeep of software has the structural signature of labor—cyclical, consumed in its own performance, leaving nothing that stands unless it is done again—without the biological substrate that made labor *labor* for Arendt. That is the sense in which the argument proceeds: not that software *is* labor, but that so much of it takes the *labor-form*, and that the trade's response to that form tells us something it has not admitted to itself.

3.3 Rot and the rotation

The labor-form has two clear instances in software, and both are worth naming concretely rather than in the abstract. The first is rot, which we have already seen: the

[2] Hannah Arendt, *The Human Condition* (University of Chicago Press, 1958), chs. III–IV. This is the whole of what the book borrows from her: the labor/work distinction, and nothing else—not action, not natality, not the public realm. The distinction is used as an instrument, and her larger political argument is left where she made it.

dependency that must be tracked, the deprecation that must be answered, the version that must be followed—not to improve the artefact but merely to keep it standing where it already stood. This is upkeep in the exact shape of Arendt's labor: effort that buys no progress, only the deferral of decay, and buys it again next quarter. The second, and the purest, is the on-call rotation. A running system is not a finished object; it is a metabolism that must be fed or it dies, and someone must be awake to feed it. The pager, the incident, the restart, the postmortem that changes little and is filed and forgotten—this is the cyclical, consumed, world-less activity Arendt described, transposed into a data centre. Nothing stands at the end of a good on-call week except the fact that the system is still running, which is the mark of labor: the reward for doing it well is that you will do it again.

3.4 The word the trade chose

Notice, then, the word the trade reached for and what the word gives away. The dominant activity of professional software is called *maintenance*, and 'maintenance' is not a neutral term. It is, almost precisely, Arendt's word for labor—the daily, cyclical keeping-in-being that leaves nothing behind and must be repeated, of which her recurring example is the housework that is undone the moment it is finished. The industry named its central work after the paradigm of labor, and then found itself puzzled that the work so named commands no prestige.[3]

But the puzzlement is the symptom. The low status of maintenance, the glamour that clings instead to the greenfield rewrite, the way 'maintainer' is worn as duty rather than announced as achievement, the quiet misery around on-call—none of these is an accident of temperament. They are the labor/work hierarchy reasserting itself inside a trade that told itself, in chapter 1's self-image, that it was pure craft: a maker of durable things, all work and no labor. The hierarchy came in with the self-image, unexamined, and it ranks the trade's own activities behind its back. Whether that ranking should be kept is a question this book refuses to answer here, because answering it well requires the join still to come in chapter 4. For now the finding is only diagnostic: the contempt is real, it is inherited, and it is aimed at the very labor-form the medium makes unavoidable.[4]

[3]And named it after labor with the proportions right. Lientz and Swanson's survey of maintenance divided it into corrective, adaptive, perfective, and preventive, and found the field spending most of its effort not on fixing what was broken but on the adaptive and perfective upkeep that keeps a working thing abreast of a moving world—the labor-form's two purest instances (*Software Maintenance Management*, 1980; the pattern is a fixture of the cost literature after Boehm, *Software Engineering Economics*, 1981). The majority of the work is the endless keeping-abreast, and it is the majority of the work that carries the least prestige.

[4]The undervaluing of maintenance against the glamour of the new is the founding observation of the 'maintenance studies' gathered around Andrew Russell and Lee Vinsel's *The Maintainers*

3.5 Where the work-form actually lives

The same scruple compels a harder question, which a careful reader will already have raised: is code an artefact in the work sense at all? A program is not much like a table. It is closer to a score or a recipe—an arrangement of instructions, not a standing thing—and one might doubt whether the labor/work distinction has any purchase on it. The doubt is well taken, and facing it yields the chapter's most useful observation. The genuinely durable things in software are not running programs. They are *descriptions*: the specification, the wire protocol, the file format, the well-defined interface. These stand across every shift of substrate precisely because they do not run—they are read, and re-implemented, and a protocol like TCP/IP has outlived not one but every early implementation of it, because the thing that endured was the description, not the code that first honoured it.[5] In software, work takes the form of the specification that outlasts its implementations; labor takes the form of keeping any one implementation alive.

One discipline on this observation, because it is the place the argument could go wrong. To say that the specification has the work-form and the deployment has the labor-form is a claim about *structure*—about which software-things stand and which must be re-enacted. It is not a claim about *worth*, and the slide from the one to the other is the imported hierarchy of section 3.4 wearing a philosopher's coat. That the maintainer's labor is labor does not make it lesser; that inference is the symptom, not the diagnosis, and the book will refuse it directly when it can. Here the point is only descriptive: if you want to make something in software that stands, you will most often be writing down a description, not shipping a process—and even that standing thing, we will see, does not close the openings, it only relocates them.

(the manifesto 'Hail the Maintainers', 2016; *The Innovation Delusion*, 2020), who read it through an ethics of care. This book shares the diagnosis and departs on its ground: the claim pressed here is not that maintenance deserves more esteem, but that its labor-form is *structural*—forced by the medium—and joined to a second, logical opening that maintenance studies does not treat. The same contempt; a different account of why it is unavoidable.

[5]The apparent counter-cases—running code that *does* persist for decades, the flight software still executing aboard a 1970s spacecraft, the old lineages deep in a working protocol stack—resolve into this account rather than against it. Such code lasts either because its world was frozen (the TEX exception of section 3.1: fixed hardware, no substrate left that can move) or because it has *ossified*, grown so load-bearing that the world routes around it instead of changing it. TCP's wire format is the second kind: too widely inspected in transit to evolve, it did not come to rest so much as harden, and the labor of change relocated to a new layer built to escape it—QUIC, carried over UDP and encrypting its transport headers precisely so it cannot be ossified in turn. The code that looks most finished is the most heroically maintained or the most rigid; neither is repose.

3.6 The maker, and the tool that vanishes

Turn last from the artefact to the one making it, because the two openings both run through her hands. The competence a good programmer has is, in Gilbert Ryle's terms, a *knowing-how* and not a *knowing-that*: it shows in the performance and cannot be reduced to a set of propositions carried in the head.[6] Taste, the feel for the tight loop, the sense that an abstraction has finally sat right—these are knowing-how, and Michael Polanyi's remark that 'we know more than we can tell' does one piece of work here and then departs: it names why craft resists full specification, and so hands straight back to chapter 2's penumbra. The reason the rule can never absorb the whole of what a skilled reviewer knows is that the knowledge is tacit, performed rather than stated; the custom that fills the rule's open texture is knowing-how, which is why it cannot simply be written down and be done with.[7]

And there is one more thing the maker's experience shows, borrowed as an observation and stripped of the philosophy that first stated it. A working tool is invisible: you see through it to the task, and are no more aware of the editor, the library, the running system than the carpenter is aware of the hammer while the nail goes in. The tool becomes conspicuous only when it breaks. Debugging is that becoming-conspicuous: the moment the bug appears, the whole web of relations the working code had kept out of sight lights up at once, and the programmer sees, suddenly and often for the first time, the world she had been dwelling inside. That a codebase is a world in this sense—a web of durable relations one inhabits and notices only when it fractures—is a fact we will need when the openings meet. Heidegger named the appearing of the broken tool; the point stands in plain terms without his ontology, and that plain form is the only one it takes in this book.[8]

3.7 Two openings, and a question

The second opening now stands beside the first, and the book has been careful to keep them apart. The rule cannot close over its cases: that was logical, and for the formal

[6] Gilbert Ryle, 'Knowing How and Knowing That' (1945) and *The Concept of Mind* (1949). Craft is knowing-how; this is the book's account of skill, and it is deliberately an analytical one, not a phenomenology.

[7] This is Peter Naur's thesis in 'Programming as Theory Building' (1985): the program is a *theory* held by the people who built it, not reducible to the code and documentation they leave behind, so a team that inherits the artefact without the theory rebuilds it from the outside and gets it wrong. The reviewing custom of section 2.4 is that theory in one of its aspects; that it dies when its holders leave is the sharpest reason the penumbra cannot be closed merely by writing things down.

[8] The observation is Heidegger's (*Being and Time*, §§15–16); it is used here purely as a description of what debugging is like, and carries none of the surrounding apparatus.

core, a theorem. The artefact cannot come to rest: that is temporal, and follows from a medium whose substrate is always moving. They are two different ways of not being finished, and their conjunction is what sets software apart. The temporal opening it does not suffer alone: every made thing in the physical world decays and asks for upkeep, and the bridge and the aircraft are maintained or they fail, so a craft that only aged would be in numerous company. What no bridge suffers is the first opening. Its design harbours no region that a procedure provably cannot decide, because a bridge computes nothing and Rice's theorem has no purchase on steel; its penumbra, such as it is, is the ordinary vagueness of any plan, not a theorem about the limits of rule. Software alone inherits both at once—the maker's durable-making impulse from chapter 1 meeting a medium that withholds completion twice over, once at the rule and once at the thing—and it is the pairing, not either opening by itself, that no older craft had to meet.

The discipline this book set itself forbids collapsing the two into one by assertion, and the promise will be kept. But it does not forbid asking whether they ever meet. Two openings can be merely side by side, two true facts about a difficult medium with nothing between them; or there can be a place where they are not two facts but one event, seen from two sides. If there is no such place, the book is two essays in a shared cover, and would say so plainly. If there is exactly one, it is the hinge on which everything turns. There is exactly one, and it is the subject of chapter 4.

Chapter 4

The Hardening

4.1 One commit

Return to the mutable default argument, which chapter 2 set among its penumbral cases and passed over in a sentence; it is a rule that no one legislated and everyone obeyed. In Python, a function may be given a default value for one of its parameters, and the default is evaluated once, when the function is defined, not once per call. So a default that happens to be a list is created a single time and then shared, silently, across every call that falls back to it:

```
def append_to(element, target=[]):
    target.append(element)
    return target
```

The second call to `append_to` does not begin with an empty list. It begins with the list the first call left behind. This is not a bug in Python; it follows exactly from the language's stated rule about when default expressions are evaluated. The language is silent on whether you *ought* to write it. For years the answer lived only in the oral culture of the language—passed in code review, in mailing-list replies, in the sigh of whoever debugged it first: *do not use a mutable default argument.* It was folklore. It bound no one. It was, in the vocabulary of this book, pure penumbra: a place the rule gave out and discretion decided.

Then, at a particular and recoverable moment, someone wrote it down as a rule a machine could apply—`pylint`'s `dangerous-default-value`, later `ruff`'s `B006`—and added it to a project's continuous integration, where it now fails the build.[1] From that commit forward, the folklore is folklore no longer. The convention that a reviewer

[1] The lint pre-dates its enforcement in any given repository; what is datable, and what matters here, is the commit that turns the rule on for a particular codebase—the line added to a

used to enforce by hand, case by case, whenever she happened to notice it, is enforced by nobody and everybody, automatically, on every change, forever.

This chapter is about that single commit, because the whole of the book meets in it. The two openings the book has been describing—the rule that cannot close over its cases (chapter 2), and the artefact that cannot be finished (chapter 3)—are not two subjects that happen to share a cover. At the moment a convention hardens into a lint rule they are one event, seen from two sides. The commit is the place they touch. Everything now turns on whether they touch as one thing genuinely does, or as two things pushed into a handshake. So the test is simple: describe the commit twice, once in each vocabulary, and see whether the same referent answers to both descriptions.

4.2 The first description: a boundary moves

Take first the vocabulary of the rule and its penumbra. Before the commit, the prohibition on mutable defaults lived in the penumbra of the language: the formal rule (the type checker, the interpreter) admitted the code without complaint, and what forbade it was an unwritten common law of the codebase, enforced by whichever human happened to be reading. It had the standing section 2.4 gave to precedent—persuasive, accreted, binding by pressure rather than by any doctrine that said it bound.

The commit changes the standing. What was penumbral custom becomes mechanically-enforced statute: no longer discretionary, no longer dependent on a reader noticing, applied by procedure to every case that falls under it. A region that lay outside the settled core—the space the language left open—has been *annexed* into the core. The boundary between what the rule decides and what it leaves to discretion has moved, and it has moved in a particular direction: outward, enclosing ground that was open before.

Two things are worth pressing here, because they are what makes software the place to study this and not merely to suffer it. The first is that the enclosure is a decision, not a discovery: nothing about the mutable default *compelled* its promotion to statute, and the neighbouring penumbra of conventions that have *not* been hardened—the Rust codebase that still leaves the discipline of its `unsafe` blocks to a reviewer's eye rather than to `clippy`—proves that the line could have been drawn elsewhere.[2] The second is that the move is *visible*. Jurisprudence can theorise the moment a line of cases crystallises into a rule, but it can never point to the instant it happened; there is no

configuration file, with an author and a timestamp. The migration this chapter describes is not the invention of the lint but its *adoption*.

[2]Compare, too, the endpoint at the far end of the same axis: Go makes an unused local variable not a lint but a *compile error*—a convention hardened past statute into the language's own constitution, no longer optional even in principle. The three cases—unwritten custom, optional lint, compile error—are one convention-type at three settled degrees of enclosure, and a language's character is largely the record of which conventions it has moved how far.

timestamp on the hardening of a common law. In software there is. The boundary's movement is a diff. It has an author, a date, and a reason in the commit message. The one thing the study of open texture has always lacked—the boundary caught in the act of moving—software supplies as a matter of routine bookkeeping.

That is the commit, described completely, in the language of rules. Nothing in the description mentions labor, craft, or the passage of the working day. Hold it, and describe the same commit again.

4.3 The second description: labor becomes work

Take now the vocabulary of the working day. Before the commit, the convention was kept alive by repetition. It existed only insofar as a reviewer re-enacted it: read the diff, recognised the pattern, left the comment, explained the footgun once more. The next pull request began with the convention un-enforced again, waiting to be re-enacted by whoever read it next. Its maintenance was cyclical and consumed in the doing—kept in being only by being done again, and leaving, at the end of each review, nothing durable behind but a merged branch and the same task waiting tomorrow. This is the labor-form exactly: not biological necessity, but its structural signature—the endless re-enactment that sustains a thing without ever setting it down.

The commit sets it down. The decision that had to be re-made every review is made once and *stands.* It is now an artefact in the world—a rule in a file, durable across every future change, enforced without anyone re-enacting it—and the reviewer who used to spend part of each day re-adjudicating mutable defaults never spends that part of a day again. A piece of what was labor, consumed in its own performance, has become work: fabricated once, lasting, added to the durable furniture of the project. And it takes the exact form chapter 3 found all durable software-work to take. What stands is not a running process but a *description*—a rule written down, read and re-applied by machine, holding across every later shift of the code beneath it just as a specification holds across its implementations. The hardening manufactures, out of a scrap of the working day, one more of the descriptions that are the only things in software that last. The reviewer's attention, freed from the case the rule now covers, is available for the cases it does not.

That is the commit, described completely, in the language of labor and work. And here is the finding the whole merger was staked on: it is the *same commit.* Not an analogy between two commits, not a parallel between two kinds of event—one line added to one configuration file, which the first description calls the annexation of penumbra into core and the second calls the conversion of labor into work. The boundary that moves outward in the first description and the labor that sets itself down as work in the second are one act under two names. The enclosure of the open region *is* the setting-down of the endless task; to make the rule stand mechanically and to relieve the day of its re-enactment are not two consequences of the commit but one consequence described in two vocabularies. The logical opening and the temporal opening, which the book has kept apart as two lenses, here fall on a single point and resolve to a single image. This is the heart the merger needed, and it is real: the join is a referent, not a resemblance.

4.4 Why it is a treadmill and not a rescue

If the chapter stopped here it would have proved too much, and would have reproduced, at the end, the very error the book was built to avoid: the fantasy that the openings can be closed. They cannot, and the same commit that seems to close a piece of them shows why.

Look at the enclosure again from the side of the rule. The lint does not abolish the penumbra; it relocates it. Every mechanical rule acquires an edge of its own—the false positive, the case that meets the letter and violates the point, the legitimate exception—and at that edge someone must again decide, by hand and without a rule, whether this is the case that does not count. The enclosure of open texture generates open texture at its own frontier: the core grows, the penumbra does not shrink, it moves outward to the fence. How far the discretion at that new fence reaches, and what it asks of whoever exercises it, is chapter 5's subject; here it is enough to see that the fence has one.

Look at the same commit from the side of the day. The convention set down as work is durable, but the codebase it governs is not finished and will not be. Fresh patterns arrive faster than anyone can harden them; each week's code raises conventions no lint yet covers, held in being only by a reviewer re-enacting them until they, in turn, are written down or forgotten. The labor converted to work at this one point is replaced by labor at others, because the artefact keeps moving and the moving is what it *is*—and a model that generates code only drives the cycle faster, emitting plausible conventions quicker than any team can write them down. Setting down one task does not end the day's re-enactment; it clears a space the next un-hardened convention fills.

So the commit is what the two descriptions found, and no more: a real enclosure, local and durable where it lands, and not for a moment final. It closes nothing. It moves a boundary and sets down a task, and both the boundary and the task re-appear a little further out. Whether the trade is any better for an enclosure that is always overtaken—whether such a commit is worth making, and what divides one worth making from one that quietly makes things worse—is the question the next chapter must take up, now that the two openings have been shown to meet. What the join establishes, and hands on, is only this: the point where the logical opening and the temporal opening touch is not a point at which either of them closes. It is a point at which both can be worked at once, by a single act—and the act, like the openings it works, does not come to an end.

Chapter 5

The Frontier Re-Opens

5.1 The edge the rule grows

The hardening of chapter 4 looked, for the length of one commit, like a closing. A piece of the penumbra was annexed into the core; a judgement that had been made by hand, case by case, became a rule a machine applies for nothing and forever. But watch the new rule for a week and its own edge appears. The lint that fences off the mutable default begins to catch cases its author never pictured: the false positive, the construction that satisfies the letter and violates the point, the legitimate exception that is the thing the rule was too coarse to see. And so every lint ships with an escape hatch—the `# noqa`, the `#[allow(...)]`, the inline suppression that says, *here the rule does not apply.* Writing that suppression is not the absence of judgement but its return. It is discretion coming back, unlegislated, to a margin the rule created by the mere fact of existing—and it is, if anything, a *larger* discretion than the one the lint replaced, because the person who writes `# noqa` overrules a machine installed precisely to bind her, on her own authority, with no procedure to consult and no reviewer necessarily watching. The penumbra of chapter 2 was not abolished by hardening. It was pushed to the fence of the new rule, where someone must again decide, by hand and without a rule, whether this is the case that does not count.

5.2 Relocation is the law

The same thing shows from the side of the day. The convention set down as work is durable, but the codebase it governs is not, and will not be; new patterns arrive faster than they can be hardened, so the labor converted to work at one point returns as labor at ten others, kept alive by re-enactment in review until it, too, is written down—if it ever is. Neither lens shows an enclosure that holds. What both show, now that they have met, is a single law of the medium: every enclosure relocates the openings and none of them shuts. Chapter 1's TEX remains the one exception, and it bought its completion the only way the exception allows, by stepping out of the medium's condition altogether; everything that stays in the medium inherits, at each hardening, a frontier that re-opens just beyond the fence it just built.

The engineering tradition has a name for the most deliberate version of this move, and it is worth meeting on its own terms, because at first it looks like a refutation. Design for change: draw the module boundary around what you expect to vary, hide the volatile decision behind an interface, and a change that would otherwise touch a hundred call sites touches one. This is not folklore but the settled counsel of the field—Parnas built information hiding out of exactly it, and told designers to modularise around anticipated change and around the extension and contraction the system would later want;[1] Meyer made it a principle; a whole school now designs for evolution as a first commitment. It works, and nothing here disputes that it works. But notice what it does in the vocabulary this book has built. To design for change is to harden *in advance*—to convert an anticipated stretch of penumbra into a boundary before the cases that would have filled it by hand arrive. It is the same enclosure the lint performed, moved earlier in time. And it relocates by the same law: the interface that absorbs a hundred edits into one is itself a decision about where variation is allowed, and the variation the designer did *not* anticipate now breaks against that boundary, at a new margin the good interface created by drawing itself. Anticipation buys enormous leverage over the change it foresaw. It buys nothing against the openness of the medium, because there is no boundary whose far side is not another frontier. Design for change is not the escape from relocation. It is relocation practised with foresight—the best the craft can do, and still not a closing.

This changes the question the book has been asking. If relocation is guaranteed, then whether to harden is no longer interesting—of course one hardens; it is the one move the double opening permits, and chapter 4 showed it is a real and worthwhile one. What is interesting is what the relocation *costs*, and that, it turns out, is not a technical question at all. Two hardenings can be identical in what they mechanise and opposite in what they leave behind, and the difference between them is where the rest of this book's argument lives.

5.3 Staffed in the open, staffed in the dark

Return for a moment to the lawyer's courtroom, which chapter 2 borrowed and then had to qualify. When a judge reaches the penumbra of a statute and finds no answer

[1] David Parnas, 'On the Criteria to Be Used in Decomposing Systems into Modules' (1972) and 'Designing Software for Ease of Extension and Contraction' (1979). Meyer's open/closed principle (*Object-Oriented Software Construction*, 1988)—modules open to extension, closed to modification—is the same counsel in a maxim, and the 'evolutionary architecture' of Ford, Parsons, and Kua (*Building Evolutionary Architectures*, 2017) is its systems-scale descendant.

there, she does what chapter 2 said she does: she supplies one. But notice the conditions under which she supplies it. She is named. She gives reasons, in an opinion written to be read. The decision enters a record others can cite, distinguish, and—on appeal—overturn. The penumbra of the law is filled, but it is filled *in the open*: the discretion is exercised where it can be seen, argued with, and held to account.

Now set the software fillers beside her. Some fill the penumbra openly enough: a convention enforced in review by a colleague who can be asked *why*, and who answers. Others do not. The optimiser that exploits an undefined behaviour makes a decisive choice about your program answerable to no one at the call site. A refactor that quietly erases an established pattern fills the penumbra by subtraction and leaves no record that a decision was made at all. And a suggestion accepted from a model trained on the accumulated custom of past code—returned instantly, fluent, usually right—fills the penumbra with the customary answer while able to give no reason it had none. These are not equally troubling because some are automated and others human. They are troubling in proportion to a single thing: whether the discretion they exercise leaves a reason that can be demanded and a record that can be read.

That is the criterion the chapter has been walking toward, and it is worth stating flatly. What distinguishes a benign relocation of the penumbra from a corrosive one is not whether the margin gets filled—it always does—nor whether the filler is a person or a program. It is whether the filling is done in the open. An enclosure is defensible to exactly the extent that the new margin it creates is staffed accountably: by someone or something that can be named, asked for a reason, and corrected on a record. Hardening that pushes discretion into the light is the craft improving itself. Hardening that pushes it into the dark is the craft mortgaging its judgement to fillers it cannot interrogate.

5.4 The filler that cannot be asked

The starkest case is not new in kind, only in degree, and seeing that keeps the argument from overstating itself. Section 2.4 already found that even a purely human customary order keeps no reporter: the reasoning behind most review decisions vanishes into stale threads no one reopens, and the precedent survives not as a citable opinion but as the code itself. The trade has long filled its penumbra with a common law that keeps almost no record. A statistical model does not introduce record-less discretion to software; it takes the last trace away. Where the human custom at least survived *as the code*, a legible artefact one could read back to reconstruct the rule, the model's custom survives only as weights: uncitable, undistinguishable, unable to be asked the reason it never formed. It is the reporter-less customary order of chapter 2 carried to its limit, and the limit is a penumbra filled at scale by something that can be neither questioned nor overruled with reasons, only accepted or declined.

It is tempting, faced with a filler that fast and that fluent, to think the closing has arrived at last—that this is the tool which finally finishes the job. The temptation should be met with the theorem of chapter 2. A model guesses over the openings; it does not shut them. Rice's result binds a learned guesser exactly as it binds a type discipline: no procedure, trained or programmed, decides an undecidable property, and no fluency about the penumbra converts a guess into a proof. So the general shape of the finding about these tools is not that they close the medium's openings but the reverse. They are the strongest demonstration the book has that nothing closes: a filler quick enough to make the permanence of the penumbra *visible*, by filling it endlessly and never once removing it. The artefact-level fact is plain enough—an AI-authored change can be merged, correct and shippable, with no one on the team able to state the reason it is right—and the danger in it is not that the code is bad. Often it is good. The danger is that a growing share of the trade's discretion comes to be exercised where no reason is left and no record is kept, which is the condition the criterion warns against.

There is one more thing to see about this filler, and it belongs to the book's other opening. A model does not fill the penumbra with just any answer; it fills it with the answer the past would have given, because the past is the whole of what it was trained on. Its fluency is the accumulated custom of chapter 3's never-finished artefacts—every legacy codebase the trade complained of maintaining—distilled into a generator of new code. And this turns software's relation to its own history inside out. Chapter 3 found the past a *burden*: the old system carried along a moving substrate, the standing debt of the labor-form. Here the same past returns as a *resource*, the corpus without which the model could not produce at all—so that the trade does not escape its history but only changes the form of its dependence on it, from maintaining the legacy artefact to being fed by the legacy corpus. There is no more setting down the second than the first. The tool that looked, a paragraph ago, like the one that might close the temporal opening is instead its deepest instance: a way of producing that cannot proceed except by consuming a past it can neither finish nor use up. And the irony is the one chapter 3 taught us to expect—the accumulated output of the upkeep the trade least honours is precisely the capital the celebrated model is built from.

5.5 Neither redemption nor betrayal

With the criterion in hand, the book's long normative wobble finally comes to rest. The argument has been pulled the whole way between two temptations. The first is that hardening *redeems* the craft—that by converting labor into lasting work it delivers, at last, the finished thing chapter 1 said the maker wanted. The second is its mirror: that hardening *betrays* the craft, that the elevation of the written rule and the durable specification is a snobbery that crowns the architect and despises the maintainer. Both are now answered, and by the same stroke.

Hardening does not redeem, because the frontier always re-opens; there is no sequence of enclosures that arrives at closure, and the belief that there is merely repeats chapter 1's memory of another workshop. But it is not betrayal either, because the labor it relieves was real and the relief is real, and—the deeper point—the labor and work hierarchy of chapter 3 was never the thing at issue. Whether the maintainer's labor ranks below the specifier's work is the wrong question, and asking it is the very symptom chapter 3 diagnosed. The right question is not about the standing of the labor but about the visibility of the discretion: not *which activity is nobler* but *is the judgement that survives every enclosure exercised where it can be seen.* The ethics of software do not live at closure, which is unavailable to everything that stays in the medium. They live at the margin, which is permanent. Not in finishing, which no one can do, but in staffing the unfinishable in the open.

This is a theme an earlier book in this series could only assert; five chapters have now earned it, deriving it from the permanence of the two openings rather than declaring it as a mood.[2]

So one question remains, and the whole book has been walking toward it. If nothing closes—if the rule never completes and the artefact never rests and every enclosure only carries the frontier a little further out—then what, exactly, is the craft, and what would it mean to do it well? The answer is not a technique. It is the endless choosing, and it is the last thing to say.

[2]The ethics of the penumbra—of who fills the gap a rule leaves, and under what light—was raised in *The Worldless Machine* (Code Crafting no. 3), which named the problem. Here it is derived, from the non-closure established in chapter 2 and chapter 3, rather than taken as given.

Conclusion: The Endless Choosing

...no course of action could be determined by a rule, because every course of action can be made out to accord with the rule.

Ludwig Wittgenstein, *Philosophical Investigations*, §201

ἔνθα καὶ ἠματίη μὲν ὑφαίνεσκεν μέγαν ἱστόν,
νύκτας δ’ ἀλλύεσκεν, ἐπεὶ δαΐδας παραθεῖτο.

By day she wove at the great loom; by night, by torchlight, she unmade what the day had made.

Homer, *Odyssey* 2.104–105

The book set out under a promise it can now keep, and a temptation it can now refuse. Chapter 5 ended by asking what is left to do, and to do well, once nothing closes—once neither the rule nor the artefact will ever come to rest. The temptation is to answer with a technique: one more discipline, one more tool, the practice that finally delivers the finished thing. That answer is the one the whole book has been earning the right to decline. There is no technique that closes the openings, because the openings are not defects that technique addresses. One is a theorem and the other is a condition of the medium, and a craft practised over them is not a craft that removes them. It is a craft that knows what it is standing on.

The half the book kept

Begin where the argument began, because the first thing to say at the end is what was never surrendered. Chapter 1 found the trade's self-image to be half right and half wrong, and the book has spent itself on the wrong half—the belief that software is a medium in which well-made things stay made. But the right half was carried the whole way, untouched, and it is the note to end on. The impulse to build something that stands—to make the abstraction sit right, to leave the module clearer than one found it, to do the work well for no reason beyond the work—is real, and it is not refuted by anything in these pages. What the book took away was not the impulse but one false consolation that had attached itself to it: that the impulse, satisfied well enough, terminates in a finished object the maker can set down and walk away from. That consolation is gone. The desire it attached to is not. A maker can want to build things that stand, and be right to want it, in a medium that never lets the standing be final—and the wanting is not made foolish by the medium's refusal, only unmoored from the completion it used to expect.

Adequate, not successful

This is the distinction the whole conclusion turns on, and five chapters have earned the right to draw it plainly where an earlier book in this series could only assert it.[3] There are two kinds of response one can make to the double opening, and the trade's unhappiness comes largely from confusing them. A *successful* response would close the opening: finish the artefact, complete the rule, arrive at the state where nothing more is required. That response is unavailable, not contingently but in principle, and every hope pinned to it curdles into the disappointment chapter 1 diagnosed—the maintainer's low morale, the perpetual sense of falling short of a line that was never reachable. An *adequate* response does not close the opening; it meets it. It sets down the fraction of the endless that can be set down, staffs the margin that setting-down reopens, and does both again tomorrow, without the fantasy that the doing will one day be over. The difference is not resignation. Resignation stops choosing; the adequate response is nothing but choosing. It is the difference between failing at an impossible task and succeeding at the possible one that stands in its place.

The choosing itself

And the possible task has, by now, an exact shape, because the book has been assembling it. It is not a disposition or an attitude but a repeated, concrete act, and both openings meet in it. From the side of the rule, to choose well is to decide which stretch of penumbra to enclose—which unwritten custom is worth hardening into a rule that stands, and which is better left to the reviewer's discretion because the cost of the en-

[3] The adequate/successful distinction closed *The Worldless Machine* (Code Crafting no. 3) as a claim about living with limits it could not fully ground. Here it is derived: from the permanence of the two openings (chapter 2, chapter 3) and the relocation that follows every enclosure (chapter 4, chapter 5), the difference between reversing a condition and answering it well is no longer a mood but a result.

closure exceeds the labor it would relieve.[4] From the side of the day, the same act sets down a piece of the endless re-enactment as durable work—and opens, at the fence it builds, a new margin that someone must now staff. And here the criterion of chapter 5 becomes the whole of what doing-it-well means: to choose well is to staff that new margin *in the open*, so that the discretion which survives every enclosure is exercised where it can be named, asked for a reason, and corrected on a record. The maker who hardens a convention and hides the exemption behind an unaccountable filler has enclosed badly, however clean the rule; the maker who hardens less but keeps the remaining discretion legible has enclosed well. The choosing is not only *what* to set down but *under what light* to leave what will not set down—and that second half is where the ethics of the craft actually live, because it is the half that is permanent.

The diff, once more

Nothing in this survives contact with the tool that seems, each time it arrives, to promise the closing at last. The fastest filler the trade has yet built—the model that returns the customary answer instantly and fluently over any stretch of penumbra—does not change the result, and it is worth saying so once more at the end so the promise is not mistaken for a refutation. It guesses over the openings; chapter 2's theorem binds it as it binds every procedure; it fills the margin endlessly and closes none of it. It is, if anything, the clearest demonstration the book has that nothing closes: a machine that makes the permanence of the penumbra visible by filling it forever and never once removing it. The question it sharpens is the only question there was—who answers for the discretion, and where is the record—and that question is not new, only newly urgent.

So the craft is the endless choosing, and this is what it means to do it well: to build, in a medium that grants the building and withholds the completion, the things that can be made to stand; to set down, commit by commit, the fraction of the never-finished that is worth setting down; and to keep in the open the margin that every setting-down re-opens. The machine is never done and the rule is never complete—not two conditions the programmer labors under, but one condition met at a single recurring act, and visible, for once and only in this medium, in the diff. Everywhere else the boundary between the settled and the open moves in the dark, with no author

[4]The choice is genuine in both directions. Not every convention should be a lint; a rule mechanised too eagerly buys its enforcement with a frontier of false positives that costs more discretion than it saved. Deciding *which* to harden, and when, is the craft—not the reflex to harden everything, which merely relocates the labor into the writing and suppressing of rules. The practitioner's name for the same choice is John Ousterhout's *strategic* versus *tactical* programming—the investment in structure that will stand against the pull of the merely-working (*A Philosophy of Software Design*, 2018); this book grounds that counsel in the two openings rather than offering it as advice.

and no date. Here it moves in the light, and can be signed. That it must be signed again tomorrow is not the defeat of the craft. It is the craft.

Bibliography

[Arendt, 1958] Arendt, H. (1958). *The Human Condition.* University of Chicago Press, Chicago. Labor/work distinction: chs. III–IV.

[Beck, 1999] Beck, K. (1999). *Extreme Programming Explained: Embrace Change.* Addison-Wesley, Reading, MA.

[Boehm, 1981] Boehm, B. W. (1981). *Software Engineering Economics.* Prentice Hall, Englewood Cliffs, NJ.

[Brooks, 1995] Brooks, Jr., F. P. (1995). *The Mythical Man-Month: Essays on Software Engineering.* Addison-Wesley, Reading, MA, anniversary edition. Orig. 1975. The anniversary edition adds "No Silver Bullet: Essence and Accidents of Software Engineering" (1986): software's essential difficulties are irreducible—not removable by any single advance in tooling. The trade's own admission, from inside engineering, that closure is not on offer.

[Ford et al., 2017] Ford, N., Parsons, R., and Kua, P. (2017). *Building Evolutionary Architectures: Support Constant Change.* O'Reilly, Sebastopol, CA.

[Hart, 1961] Hart, H. L. A. (1961). *The Concept of Law.* Oxford University Press, Oxford. Core-and-penumbra picture: ch. VII.

[Heidegger, 1962] Heidegger, M. (1962). *Being and Time.* Harper & Row, New York. Trans. Macquarrie and Robinson; the ready-to-hand / broken tool is §§15–16. Orig. *Sein und Zeit*, 1927.

[Hunt and Thomas, 1999] Hunt, A. and Thomas, D. (1999). *The Pragmatic Programmer: From Journeyman to Master.* Addison-Wesley, Reading, MA. A founding text of the "software craftsmanship" self-image; cited in Ch. 1 as an exhibit of that self-image, not as a source.

[Knuth, 1968] Knuth, D. E. (1968). *The Art of Computer Programming.* Addison-Wesley, Reading, MA. Multi-volume; in progress since 1968, still unfinished.

[Knuth, 1986] Knuth, D. E. (1986). *TEX: The Program*, volume B of *Computers & Typesetting*. Addison-Wesley, Reading, MA. The complete source of TEX, published as a literate program in WEB.

[Lehman, 1980] Lehman, M. M. (1980). Programs, life cycles, and laws of software evolution. *Proceedings of the IEEE*, 68(9):1060–1076. The First Law, "Continuing Change".

[Lehman and Belady, 1985] Lehman, M. M. and Belady, L. A. (1985). *Program Evolution: Processes of Software Change.* Academic Press, London.

[Lientz and Swanson, 1980] Lientz, B. P. and Swanson, E. B. (1980). *Software Maintenance Management.* Addison-Wesley, Reading, MA. Corrective / adaptive / perfective / preventive; the latter two dominate.

[Meyer, 1988] Meyer, B. (1988). *Object-Oriented Software Construction.* Prentice Hall, New York. The open/closed principle.

[Morris, 1885] Morris, W. (1885). *Useful Work versus Useless Toil.* Socialist League Office, London.

[Naur, 1985] Naur, P. (1985). Programming as theory building. *Microprocessing and Microprogramming*, 15(5):253–261. The program as a theory in its makers' heads, irreducible to code and documentation; the software-specific ancestor of Ch. 3's knowing-how account of the reviewing custom.

[Ousterhout, 2018] Ousterhout, J. (2018). *A Philosophy of Software Design.* Yaknyam Press, Palo Alto, CA. Prescriptive strand. Complexity is incremental and accumulates (a Lehman echo, Ch. 3); "strategic" vs. "tactical" programming—investing in durable structure against the pull of the merely-working (Conclusion).

[Parnas, 1972] Parnas, D. L. (1972). On the criteria to be used in decomposing systems into modules. *Communications of the ACM*, 15(12):1053–1058. Information hiding; modules drawn around anticipated changes.

[Parnas, 1979] Parnas, D. L. (1979). Designing software for ease of extension and contraction. *IEEE Transactions on Software Engineering*, SE-5(2):128–138.

[Parnas, 1994] Parnas, D. L. (1994). Software aging. In *Proceedings of the 16th International Conference on Software Engineering (ICSE)*, pages 279–287. IEEE.

[Polanyi, 1966] Polanyi, M. (1966). *The Tacit Dimension.* Doubleday, Garden City, NY. "We know more than we can tell": p. 4.

[Rice, 1953] Rice, H. G. (1953). Classes of recursively enumerable sets and their decision problems. *Transactions of the American Mathematical Society*, 74(2):358–366.

[Ruskin, 1853] Ruskin, J. (1853). The nature of gothic. In *The Stones of Venice*, volume 2. Smith, Elder & Co., London.

[Russell and Vinsel, 2020] Russell, A. L. and Vinsel, L. (2020). *The Innovation Delusion: How Our Obsession with the New Has Disrupted the Work That Matters Most.* Currency, New York. The book-length statement of 'maintenance studies'; cited in Ch. 3 as the nearest company to this book's diagnosis of maintenance's low status, from which it departs on grounding.

[Ryle, 1945] Ryle, G. (1945). Knowing how and knowing that. *Proceedings of the Aristotelian Society*, 46:1–16.

[Ryle, 1949] Ryle, G. (1949). *The Concept of Mind.* Hutchinson, London.

[Sennett, 2008] Sennett, R. (2008). *The Craftsman.* Yale University Press, New Haven.

[Waismann, 1945] Waismann, F. (1945). Verifiability. *Proceedings of the Aristotelian Society, Supplementary Volumes*, 19:119–150.

[Wittgenstein, 1953] Wittgenstein, L. (1953). *Philosophical Investigations.* Blackwell, Oxford. Trans. G. E. M. Anscombe; the rule-following remarks are §§185–242.

Index

Colophon

Produced with LaTeX compiled by Tectonic (XeTeX),
normalised for print with Ghostscript.

Typeset in Linux Libertine.
Printed on 90 gsm FSC-certified matte paper
sourced from responsibly managed forests.

Written with the assistance of large language models—
tools subordinate to judgment, not a replacement for it.

The build is green.

It will not stay green.